AF430271

ISTQB Certified Advanced Level Technical Test Analyst Exam Practice Questions & Dumps

Exam Practice Questions for ISTQB ATTA LATEST VERSION

Presented By: Vector Books

About Vector Books:

Vector Books is a publishing house based in Houston, Texas, USA, a platform that is available both online & locally, which unleashes the power of educational content, literary collection, poetry & many other book genres. We make it easy for writers & authors to get their books designed, published, promoted, and sell professionally on worldwide scale with eBook + Print delivery. Vector Books was founded in 2015, and is now distributing books internationally.

Note: Find answers of the questions at the last of the book.

QUESTION 1
An embedded software company is considering to improve the quality of
its software components to be delivered to the integration team. After
studying various experience papers that report a higher level of quality for
software components, two main alternative techniques are identified: static
analysis and dynamic analysis. In deciding which one is most applicable
and how they relate to each other a detailed study is performed.
Which of the following are TWO key similarities between static analysis
and dynamic analysis?

A. Both are performed using requirements as its major input document
B. Both are usually undertaken by integration testers
C. Both are usually undertaken by development during coding and unit
   testing
D. Both are related to reviews
E. Both usually use a tool

QUESTION 2
Which of the following is a dynamic analysis technique related to
improving application performance?

A. Code complexity analysis
B. Profiling
C. Network package sniffing
D. Spelling and grammar checking

QUESTION 3
Definition-use pairs are identified during which of the following static
analysis activities?

A. Control flow analysis
B. Data flow activities
C. Coding standards analysis
D. Cyclomatic complexity analysis

QUESTION 4

If we say that a set of tests has achieved 100% structural decision coverage on a particular module in a program, what does that mean?

A. That all bugs present in that module were necessarily revealed by those tests.

B. That every control flow branch had been executed at least once by those tests.

C. That every dataflow in that module was exercised at least once by those tests.

D. That every path through that module was exercised at least once by those tests.

QUESTION 5

If you are flying with an economy ticket, there is a possibility that you may get upgraded to business class, especially if you hold a gold card in the airline's frequent flier program. If you don't hold a gold card, there is a possibility that you will get 'bumped' off the flight if it is full and you check in late. This is shown in the figure hereafter. Note that each box (i.e. statement) has been numbered.

Three tests have been run:

Test 1: Gold card holder who gets upgraded to business class Test 2: Non-gold card holder who stays in economy
Test 3: A person who is bumped from the flight

What is the statement coverage of these three tests?

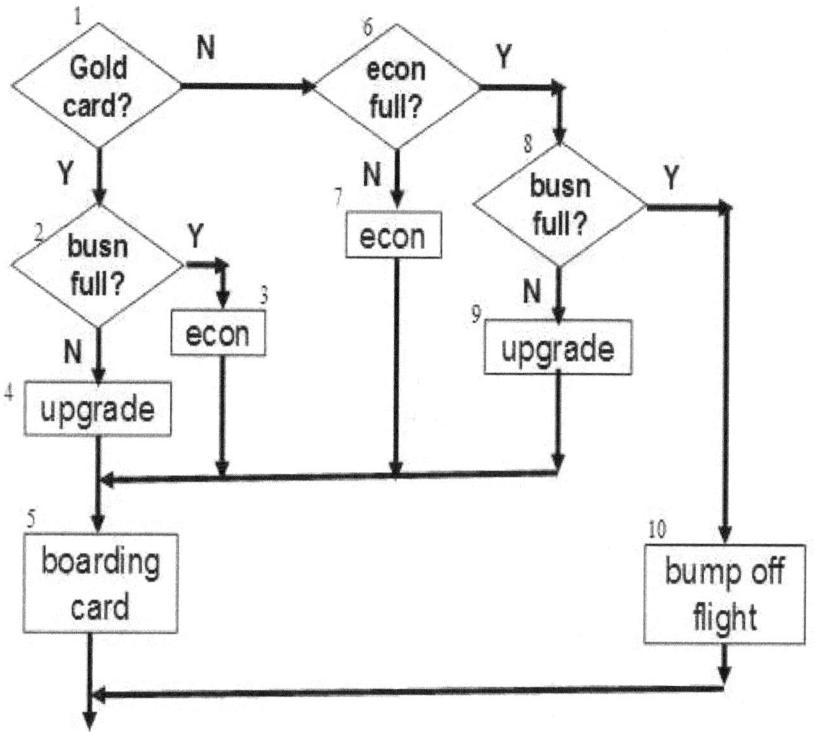

A. 60%
B. 70%
C. 80%
D. 90%

QUESTION 6

As part of a risk analysis, technical risks are analyzed. Which TWO factors influence technical risk?

A. Complexity of technology
B. Frequency of use of the affected failure
C. Interfacing and integration issues
D. Damage to image
E. Lack of reasonable workaround

QUESTION 7
A component has been analyzed as being highly critical. Which of the
following structure-based test design techniques provides the highest level
of coverage?

A. Statement testing
B. Decision testing
C. Condition determination testing
D. Multiple condition testing

QUESTION 8
The result of a product risk analysis performed on components I, II and III

of the airplane control system shows the following risk matrix:

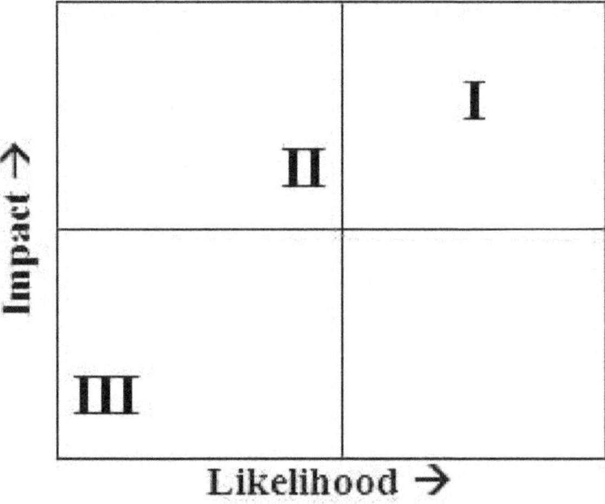

The project wants to mitigate the risks by defining different types of
coverage depending on the risk level of the components. Which of the
following would be a meaningful solution for setting the coverage targets?

A. I: Condition determination coverage, II: Decision Coverage, III:
    Statement coverage
B. I: Condition determination coverage, II: Statement coverage, III:
    Decision coverage
C. I: Decision coverage, II: Condition determination coverage, III:
    Statement Coverage
D. I: Multiple condition coverage, II: Decision coverage, III: Condition
    determination coverage

QUESTION 9

Consider the following fault attack: "Force all possible incoming errors from the software/OS interfaces to the application". Which of the following is the kind of failure you are looking for when using this attack?

A. Application crashes when unsupported characters are pasted into an input field using the windows clipboard
B. Front page of the application has incorrect spelling of the company name
C. Application fails to display financial numbers in the correct currency format in reports
D. Application miscalculates total monthly balance due on credit cards

QUESTION 10

How many test cases would be needed to achieve 100% decision coverage?

A. 1
B. 2
C. 3
D. 4

QUESTION 11

How many test cases would be needed to achieve 100% statement coverage?

A. 1
B. 2
C. 3
D. 4

QUESTION 12

What is the number of nested levels for the code fragment?

A. 0
B. 1
C. 2
D. 3

QUESTION 13
The comment frequency of the code fragment is 13%. To which ISO 9126 quality attribute does a good level of comment frequency especially contribute?

A. Portability
B. Maintainability
C. Usability
D. Efficiency

QUESTION 14
Which specification-based technique could be used to enhance coverage for this code fragment?

A. Boundary value analysis
B. Exploratory testing
C. State transition testing
D. Use case testing

QUESTION 15
Consider the following code fragment

If (a>b) and (b>c) then b = (a+c)/2
endif

Assume that in the following options, each of the three numbers in parenthesis represent the inputs for a test case, where the first number represents variable "a", the second number represents variable "b", and the third number represents variable "c".

Which of the following gives a set of test case inputs that achieves 100%

decision coverage for this fragment of code with the minimum number of

test cases? A. (5, 3, 2)
B. (5, 3, 2); (5, 4, 0)
C. (5, 4, 0); (4, 5, 0)
D. (4, 5, 0); (5, 4, 5)

QUESTION 16

For the control flow, what is the correct labelling?

i	ii	iii
A. Nodes	Link	Region
B. Nodes	Region	Link
C. Region	Link	Nodes
D. Region	Nodes	Link

QUESTION 17

Which of the following is a valid way to calculate the cyclomatic complexity?

A. Number of decisions + 2

B. Number of enclosed regions - 1

C. Number of statements - 2

D. Links - Nodes + 2

QUESTION 18

The developers have suggested test set A is adequate to test the program opposite:

Test Set A		
Test Case 1	Test case 2	Test case 3
Price = 0.1	Price = 2.0	Price = 10.0
Quantity = 1000	Quantity = 500	Quantity = 120
Bonus = 9	Bonus = 1	Bonus = 3
Market = "USA"	Market = "UK"	Market = "FRA"

When executing test set A through the program which statements are exercised?

A. All
B. All, but statement 22
C. All, but statement 27, 28 and 29
D. All, but statement 22, 27, 28 and 29

QUESTION 19

What is the value of statement coverage achieved by test case 1 from test set A?

A. ? 75% (21/28)
B. ? 78% (22/28)
C. ? 85% (24/28)
D. ? 90% (25/28)

QUESTION 20

Which additional set of test cases is needed to achieve both 100% statement coverage and 100% decision coverage?

A.

Price	Quantity	Bonus	Market
4.0	1100	1	UK
1.0	3	4	NL

B.

Price	Quantity	Bonus	Market
1.2	2000	10	USA
3.0	1100	20	UK

C.

Price	Quantity	Bonus	Market
2.0	5000	3	NL
3.0	500	3	USA

D.

Price	Quantity	Bonus	Market
5.0	1100	1	USA
1.0	1	1	USA

QUESTION 21
Which TWO additional structure-based test design techniques could be
used to dynamically test the code?

A. Condition testing
B. Multiple condition testing
C. Equivalence partitioning
D. Cause/effect graphing
E. Code reviews

QUESTION 22
How many test cases are needed to test code fragment lines 26 – 32 to
achieve 100% condition determination coverage?

A. 2
B. 3
C. 4
D. 5

QUESTION 23
The application of multiple condition testing is also being considered.

Which specification-based technique is largely based on the principle of
multiple condition testing?

A. Equivalence Partitioning
B. State Transition Testing
C. Decision Table Testing
D. Use Cases

QUESTION 24
How many test cases are needed to test code fragment lines 26 – 32 to
achieve 100% multiple condition coverage?

A. 2
B. 3
C. 4
D. 8

QUESTION 25

The Bonus Program is perceived by management to be critical. Defects in the program would almost immediately lead to financial loss. In the past an improvement program has been run to implement review based on IEEE 1028. Knowledge and skills on both formal and informal reviews are available. There is also an existing pool of review leaders. Which of the following review types would you choose to review the program?

A. Informal review

B. Inspection

C. Walkthrough

D. Management review

QUESTION 26

You have tested the program and have found that with "bonus" a boundary value has not been implemented according to design. You have written an incident report. Which of the following is the incident report of the highest quality?

A. Description: Boundary value not correctly implemented Priority: High
   Repeatability: Yes Tester: WVU
   Test case: 35 (test specification "bonus program"), V1.2

B. Description: Boundary value not correctly implemented for bonus
   Priority: Medium
   Tester: WVU
   Test case: 35 (test specification "bonus program")

C. Description: Boundary value not correctly implemented for bonus (line
   26: 10 according to design, now 5 implemented) Priority: High
   Repeatability: Yes Tester: WVU
   Test case: 35 (test specification "bonus program"), V1.2

D. Description: Boundary value not correctly implemented for bonus
   Priority: High
   Repeatability: Yes Tester: WVU
   Test case: 35 (test specification "bonus program"), V1.2

QUESTION 27
When performing code reviews, which of the following defect types will be most difficult to find?

A. Dead code
B. Variable used that is not defined
C. Memory issues
D. Conformance to design

QUESTION 28
During code reviews, it is the author's responsibility...

A. to address all major and minor defects as stated in the defect log
B. to fix all major and minor defects as stated in the defect log
C. to take action on only improvement suggestions from the defect log
D. to correct source documents that have major defects

QUESTION 29
An organisation has already implemented a static analysis tool and is considering whether code reviews would have any added value. Which of the following defect types can only be found by means of code reviews?

A. Conformance to coding standards
B. Conformance to design
C. Endless loop
D. Cyclomatic complexity too high

QUESTION 30
To support code reviews a checklist will be developed. Which TWO questions from the list would you implement as part of the code review checklist?

A. Are any magic numbers (numeric literals) used, other than 0 or 1?
B. Can each item be implemented with the techniques, tools, and resources available?
C. Is it possible during acceptance testing to verify whether the item has been satisfied?
D. Is the item specified in an exact, unambiguous way?
E. Is there any logic containing no statements and no as to why it is empty?

QUESTION 31
Applying exploratory testing (ET) during unit testing is being considered.
Which ET deliverable would be the primary candidate for informal
reviews?

A. Test log & coverage outline
B. Test charter
C. Heuristics
D. Test case specification

QUESTION 32
Which of the following is the most important benefit of making exploratory
testing part of your test approach for the "Bonus Program"?

A. The ability to utilize a very experienced test team
B. The ability to accurately predict the residual risk prior to delivery
C. The ability to prevent defects during requirements analysis
D. The ability to test effectively without a complete test basis

QUESTION 33
What are the TWO most significant benefits a test execution tool should
bring to the organisation?

A. Less expensive and time consuming regression testing
B. More structured incident management
C. Improved control and monitoring
D. Visibility on test coverage
E. More coverage during regression testing

QUESTION 34
What are the TWO most significant pitfalls the organisation should be
aware of?

A. Lack of good process as a baseline
B. Cost of maintenance of test scripts
C. Test management will become more time-consuming
D. Need to train testers and gain skills

E. Coverage measurements are often difficult

QUESTION 35
Select TWO solutions how the team could achieve significant benefits in
the use of this tool within the next 6 months?

A. Introduce data-driven or keyword driven scripting techniques
B. Change the development process
C. Select and implement a test management tool to complement the test
    suite
D. Identify critical parts of the system and concentrate on automating
    some of those tests for that particular area
E. Get business testers involved in the automation process

QUESTION 36
A developer has spent three days looking at a system that crashes now
and then. The problem was caused by two coding faults:

i. A variable was being used but had not been defined; ii.There was a
'goto' statement to an undefined label

A. Static analysis tool
B. Code coverage tool
C. Dynamic analysis tool
D. Test execution tool

QUESTION 37
A new web site has been launched for a conference organisation. There
are a number of links to other related websites for information purposes.
Customers like the new site but complaints are being made that some (not
all) of the links to other sites do not work.

A. Performance tool
B. Hyperlink tool
C. Usability testing tool
D. Static analysis tool

QUESTION 38

It has been decided to improve the efficiency and effectiveness of unit testing by acquiring a number of test tools. Which TWO of the following tools would you select to support unit testing?

A. Dynamic analysis
B. Review tool
C. Coverage measurement tool
D. Monitoring
E. Test management

QUESTION 39

You have been asked to select a number of tools to support the performance testing. Which TWO of the following tools would you recommend?

A. Test management tool
B. Load testing tool
C. Static analysis tool
D. Monitoring tool
E. Test oracle tool

QUESTION 40

At which test level would performance testing most likely be performed?

A. Component Testing
B. Integration Testing
C. System Testing
D. User Acceptance Testing

QUESTION 41
To address reliability a number of measures will be taken throughout the development and testing process. Select TWO appropriate measures that are typically taken as part of reliability engineering and/or testing of an application.

A. Define Operational Profiles
B. State Transition Testing
C. Usability testing
D. Perform design FMEAs

E. Exploratory test

ANSWER

1) Correct Answer: CE
Section: Test Techniques various
2) Correct Answer: B
Section: Test Techniques various
3) Correct Answer: B
Section: Test Techniques various
4) Correct Answer: B
Section: Test Techniques various
5) Correct Answer: C
Section: Test Techniques various
6) Correct Answer: AC
Section: Test Techniques various
7) Correct Answer: C
Section: Test Techniques various
8) Correct Answer: A
Section: Test Techniques various
9) Correct Answer: A
Section: Test Techniques various
10) Correct Answer: A
Section: Structure-based Techniques
11) Correct Answer: A
Section: Structure-based Techniques
12) Correct Answer: C
Section: Structure-based Techniques
13) Correct Answer: A
Section: Structure-based Techniques
14) Correct Answer: A
Section: Structure-based Techniques
15) Correct Answer: C
Section: Structure-based Techniques
16) Correct Answer: A
Section: Structure-based Techniques
17) Correct Answer: A
Section: Structure-based Techniques
18) Correct Answer: A
Section: Structure-based Techniques
19) Correct Answer: A
 Section: Bonus Program

20) Correct Answer: C
Section: Bonus Program
21) Correct Answer: AB
 Section: Bonus Program
22) Correct Answer: B
Section: Bonus Program
23) Correct Answer: C
 Section: Bonus Program
24) Correct Answer: D
Section: Bonus Program
25) Correct Answer: B
 Section: Bonus Program
26) Correct Answer: C
 Section: Bonus Program
27) Correct Answer: C
Section: Bonus Program
28) Correct Answer: A
Section: Bonus Program
29) Correct Answer: B
Section: Bonus Program
30) Correct Answer: AE
Section: Bonus Program
31) Correct Answer: B
 Section: Bonus Program
32) Correct Answer: D
 Section: Bonus Program
33) Correct Answer: AE
Section: Test tools & Automation
34) Correct Answer: BD
Section: Test tools & Automation
35) Correct Answer: AD
Section: Test tools & Automation
36) Correct Answer: A
Section: Test tools & Automation
37) Correct Answer: B
Section: Test tools & Automation
38) Correct Answer: AC
Section: Test tools & Automation
39) Correct Answer: BD
 Section: Testing of Software Characteristics
40) Correct Answer: C
 Section: Testing of Software Characteristics
41) Correct Answer: AD
 Section: Testing of Software Characteristics

www.ingramcontent.com/pod-product-compliance
Lightning Source LLC
Chambersburg PA
CBHW060232170726
48004CB00004BA/1525